THE
PURSUIT
OF
HAPPINESS

OTHER BOOKS BY THE AUTHOR

The Future of Democracy:
Lessons From the Past and Present
To Guide us on our Path Forward
(2016)

The Death of Democracy
(2018)

Truth & Democracy: Truth As A Guide For Personal
And Political Action In An Age Of Polarization
(2020)

Everyday Spirituality for Everyone
(2021)

Guide to Living in a Democracy
(2022)

THE
PURSUIT
OF
HAPPINESS

Steve Zolno

REGENT PRESS
Berkeley, California

ISBN 10: 1-58790-648-1
ISBN 13: 978-1-58790-648-0

Library of Congress Control Number: 2023933856

COVER IMAGE: Against an inky black backdrop, the blue swirls of spiral galaxy NGC 6956 stand out radiantly. NGC 6956 is a barred spiral galaxy, a common type of spiral galaxy with a bar-shaped structure of stars in its center. This galaxy exists 214 million light-years away in the constellation Delphinus. *[Image courtesy of NASA]*

Manufactured in the U.S.A.
REGENT PRESS
Berkeley, Californian
www.regentpress.net

CONTENTS

INTRODUCTION

The best and most beautiful things in the world cannot be seen or even touched — they must be felt with the heart – HELEN KELLER

Many of us believe that something is missing in our lives. Words come to mind like happiness, joy, contentment, peace of mind. We can't easily describe what we seek, but want to return to the feeling of well-being it seems we have lost.

That feeling is the underlying intent in our relationships, work, leisure and every other realm of our lives. We are most free to pursue it when our basic needs such as food, shelter, and clothing are met, but even in times of greatest need we still long for it.

We believe that if our world was the way we want it to be our lives would be complete and we would experience satisfaction. This is the human condition by which we perpetually put what we most want into the future. We then blame others, the world, ourselves or perhaps a force outside of us for depriving us of what we believe is our due.

Our assumption that the peace of mind we seek is in the future is what keeps it out of our grasp in the present. When we experience contentment it is because we allow it to ourselves. Happiness is the state where we no longer seek it. Thus our perennial pursuit is bound to fail.

We can learn to identify what we seek and bring it into our lives. We become more skilled at this as we begin to understand that we only can partake of happiness in the moment. This is perhaps the most difficult idea to grasp because human nature has evolved to be in a state of perpetual seeking. What our times of experiencing happiness have in common is that we momentarily stop chasing it.

Our inability to appreciate and dwell in the present has its costs in chronic stress and anxiety. Dwelling on concepts from our past causes us to fail to live in the moment. The views we carry with us cause us to miss much of what happens around and within us. This impedes our ability to interact with the world.

Paying greater attention to what is around us allows us to see more clearly and begin to move beyond our preconceptions. We can learn to base our views on what we observe rather than what we fear or fantasize. Our actions become more attuned to reality. Seeing the limits of our concepts enhances our sense of appreciation for others and our world.

We became seekers of knowledge because it led to our success as a species. In our efforts to improve our lives we developed skills to understand our surroundings and survive in increasingly challenging circumstances. We have transformed our world. But in our emphasis on survival we often ignore the negative effects of actions that create threats to ourselves and the environment that sustains us. As we gain more awareness of the results of our actions our ability to experience happiness becomes enhanced.

We want a perfect world with perfect people and hold out for them to meet our expectations. This has historical implications. The result has been anger and wars that dominate human interactions and history right up to the present. But we have the ability to move beyond the tribal mindset that dominates us. We can learn to identify and allow ourselves the experience of happiness, and then bring that into our interactions.

Some types of governments are more suited to allowing people to pursue happiness than others. Democracy – when it lives up to its promise of "rule by the people" – is the form of government most likely to enhance human fulfillment. But there are democratic and autocratic elements in us all. When we act on our democratic impulse of respect for every human being – and move our nations in that direction – our pursuit of happiness is more likely to succeed. When we succumb to our autocratic side we harm ourselves as we dwell on blame rather than progress.

Happiness is more than just a concept. It is our most basic feeling that many of us deny ourselves throughout much of our lives. It is the essential element of our nature that supersedes our concepts. We miss it most of the time because we have learned to place conditions on allowing ourselves to experience it.

I have been a teacher of children and adults for 50 years. My impression of the human condition and potential is based on that experience. I continually have expressed faith that we all have the ability to bring a greater sense of fulfillment to ourselves by directly identifying and acting on what we most seek. What I see is that happiness is our natural state and we often deny it to our detriment as we place conditions on our ability to experience it.

The chapters that follow describe how we defeat ourselves in our search for fulfilment by the views we have adopted. They also emphasize how we can become more aware of the way we frame our reality and use that awareness to move closer to the world and lives we seek. Each section is a separate essay – they can be read individually or in one sitting.

– Steve Zolno
February, 2023
Oakland, California

CERTAINTY AND UNCERTAINTY

If we discover a complete theory, it should in time be understandable by everyone, not just by a few scientists. Then we shall all, philosophers, scientists and just ordinary people, be able to take part in the discussion of the question of why it is that we and the universe exists. If we find the answer to that, it would be the ultimate triumph of human reason – for then we should know the mind of God – STEPHEN HAWKING

Early in life we search for knowledge that will enable us to get our needs met. We seek certainty so we can know what is true and how to act. We rely on those we trust to provide us guidance.

Our ability to store and use information exceeds all other creatures, which has led to the dominance of humanity over the earth. Relying on the views of others spares us the burden of considering numerous options to come to our own conclusions. This generally has worked well. We have developed knowledge and traditions that allowed our civilizations to thrive. But in our search for certainty we often settle on incomplete views; our actions fail to take the larger picture into account.

Within every culture there is an agreed set of ideas about what is true and how we should act. Our beliefs evolve slowly as experience and evidence force us to consider new information. This has allowed us to work together toward improving our knowledge and lives, but it also has been detrimental when we fail to pay attention to the evidence around us.

Five hundred years ago Europeans believed that the earth was the center of the universe because God's creation focused on the human story as told in the Bible. Those who challenged this article of faith were persecuted by the Church. If people dared believe that our planet was only one of many that revolved around the sun it would undo the idea of our special creation. This affected the way people saw their lives and even how science interpreted its observations. But that assumption was reversed with time as more scientists considered evidence rather than beliefs.

So how do we know what is true?

Most of our actions are geared toward identifying and living a successful lifestyle. Our efforts focus on supporting a career and way of life to attain the standards of our culture.

Our assumptions guide our everyday actions. We think we know much about our family and friends, our schools and work, what we must do to earn a living, and what will make us happy. We have ideas about what and who to trust and avoid. Most of us believe that individual success in a number of areas – career, finance, family, among others – will lead to our ultimate satisfaction.

In the United States – probably the most dominant culture in the world – our idea of what constitutes success has evolved over time. Our certainty about how one should act has changed. In the 1950s, when I was brought up, the predominant model of a happy family in the public eye was a smiling white group of four that included a mother, father, boy and girl. Over time a more diverse model emerged that includes people of color, one or multiple parents, and individuals of various sexual orientations. But the assumption that children can achieve greater financial status and security than their parents has evaporated amidst economic downturns.

In today's world the model for personal success has become much less clear. There seems to be no consistent standard for how to lead a successful life. The contentment we assume will be ours from pursuing a chosen vocation or lifestyle no longer seems within reach for many. We live in an age of anxiety for those who see no viable path forward, often our youth. Our search for certainty seems stymied at a time when nothing is guaranteed.

So how do we know what to believe or which path to pursue to bring long-term success and contentment? Is the idea of a clear route toward happiness and self-worth obsolete? Do we need to continually recreate ourselves as the cultural standards around us shift?

One possibility is taking a step back to realize that perhaps the compass we adopted to guide our way needs to be adjusted. Maybe the truths we assumed need to be reexamined. But how do we know where and how to readjust?

If we compare the amount of satisfaction we experience with what we thought our lifestyle and activities would bring, I think it fair to say that for most of us satisfaction falls short. We have done what we believed would make our lives complete. We've sought financial security and pursued relationships we hoped would bring stability. We've engaged in leisure activities we assumed would lead to satisfaction. But somehow our pursuits have come up short of providing the long-term contentment for which we hoped.

Perhaps the expectations we adopted from our culture no longer are viable, if they ever were. There always have been those who challenged the dominant assumptions about what leads to an actual experience of success. If we look more closely at the results of our search for a satisfying life we may find that our assumptions have betrayed us or just been incorrect. But changing the premises by which we guide our lives may be difficult – if not impossible – for most of us.

One possibility – which may seem radical – would be to put aside our assumptions of what works and reexamine what, if anything, actually does work to bring happiness. Perhaps more importantly, can we even identify what, at the core of our being, we have been searching for? And do we have the courage, at least temporarily, to set aside the assumptions we have taken on from our culture as to what leads to success? And even more bravely, do we dare to reexamine what success might be?

If we attempt this we might find that the right words to describe our ultimate goal are hard to come by. We know something is missing and have used terms that are common in our culture for what seems to be the direction we have been heading all our lives; success, happiness, contentment and a long list of others. At our core we know that words don't adequately describe what we seek because that is a dynamic feeling that defies easy description. In the course of our daily lives it seems we are limited to a choice of terms based on the past, but they fall short of describing what we really pursue.

There is much written in books and articles about something called mindfulness and how that can improve our lives. But mindfulness is just another word. Does it indicate a practice or way of life that can move us toward an understanding or realization of our real goal?

Another possibility is putting aside – even for a moment – our idea about what we seek and just allowing ourselves to consider what that really might be if we altogether leave words behind. We might find a quiet place within that seeks recognition and where words rarely penetrate.

We all came into this world in touch with that place and then sought to return to it by the use of words that never quite were adequate. But now we might decide if – or how – to allow ourselves to re-experience it. We may be describing a place beyond words, but that does not mean it doesn't exist. It may in fact be our genuine reality as words fail to adequately describe the experience or feeling we seek.

If we can recognize and dwell in that place

– even momentarily – we may begin to realize that the world we have been taught to believe in doesn't match the one of our experience. The possibility here is learning to see the world closer to the way it is and less in the way we have framed it. We may begin to see our uncertainty more as a blessing than as a curse. And this may lead to a type of certainty that supersedes our descriptions and brings us closer to a sense of genuine understanding.

Perhaps this is our real self.

CONNECTION AND ISOLATION

Where there is peace and meditation, there is neither anxiety nor doubt – FRANCIS OF ASSISI

We enter the earth from the viewpoint of connection to all that is around us. Despite what we are taught, interconnection is reality, although we live most of our lives from the perspective of separateness.

We long to re-experience that connection, which we may find in relationships and other situations when we believe that our most essential self is recognized. But no words – including those you read here – can bring us that experience. It only happens when we are willing to bring a recognition of our validity as human beings to ourselves. Allowing ourselves to go through what we are feeling eventually moves us to a different place.

In this moment we can move toward experiencing the connection we seek. We do this by envisioning it rather than assuming we are separate. We ask ourselves what happens to us during that connection: what it feels like, how we breathe, how our bodies experience it. With this kind of practice we can begin to bring it to ourselves when we choose.

Some people might believe that the experience of connection to others doesn't work in the real world, which is competitive, and that when we fail to keep our distance others can take advantage of us. But we continually are making a choice about whether to enter into the state of mind we seek or abandon it to the ways of thinking we have learned. We still can maintain our sense of connection as we remain aware that most people operate from a view of separateness. As we remain grounded in that view we can play the game of competitiveness and be less affected by the moods and actions of others. The result is joyful participation in life.

If others try to harm us, paying attention can allow us to engage in a defense based on the reality of the situation rather than total reaction. We can witness the isolated state of others without being critical or judgmental. We can compete to the utmost of our ability while understanding that the results will not affect our experience of happiness because we already know how to return to the state we seek.

Many of us have limited our vulnerability due to past disappointment and protect ourselves because we believe we haven't had our emotional needs met. We find it better to hedge our bets in interactions rather than settle for what we fear will be a repeat of past disappointments. But when we do this, we also choke off the feeling we want. As we learn to maintain our sense of connection we become less dependent on others. We experience the range of emotions we left behind long ago.

But to have the fullness of the feeling we seek, we need to allow ourselves vulnerability to others. We did this as children. Our moods varied before we learned to assume the role of consistency. But when anchored in knowing who we really are – a being with a stable connection to all that exists – we become more fully human.

When we allow ourselves the full range of our emotions they no longer seem to threaten our existence. We begin to see the moods that people go through are universal and therefore forgivable. We allow them to express their reactions without meeting our ideas of how we think they should act. And as we provide forgiveness for others we experience it for ourselves.

When we allow our range of emotions to flow through us they become validated and we no longer feel an urgent need to express them. We no longer act on our anger and passions as we experience the universality of what it means to be human. We no longer need to fight and go to war to validate who we are.

We can allow our moment-to-moment experience to flow through us – no matter how high or how low – when we are comfortable with who we are. There no longer is one way we need to be or feel but allow what comes up to go through us as it occurs. We become more comfortable with ourselves and others become more comfortable around us.

True happiness is being with the ongoing

reality of ourselves and others no matter where that takes us. As we do this we return to our essential sense of who we are.

CONCEPT AND EXPERIENCE

Let every feeling happen to you – no feeling is final
– RAINER MARIA RILKE

There is a huge gap between the concept of happiness and its experience.

We may think we know what happiness is and what leads to it. But thinking about it and actually living and breathing it are as different as reading about and participating in an adventure.

People may tell themselves that their lives are happy and nothing more is needed. Others might believe that happiness always is in some other time or place. But these pale with the dynamic experience we left behind and to which we long to return.

Our idea of happiness is a faint memory of a time we once knew when we were totally involved in interaction with the world at all levels of our being. We learned to cut that feeling off to participate in dialogue that is the way most of us communicate with others.

But the experience of real happiness is the reaction within each of us that fully engages all we encounter. If we watch small children we see they do not hold back what they feel and in how they interact with the world. Their entire selves are involved in their interaction with what is around them. They operate in the moment as they have not yet learned to imitate the social distancing of the adults around them. This is why most adults enjoy their company.

It is said that a picture is worth a thousand words. But it is not an exaggeration to say that the experience of happiness is worth a thousand pictures. No words or pictures can convey the total immersion of our being in our interactions. When truly happy we feel that our value as human beings is at least temporarily restored. The judgments we have incorporated from our past are lifted for a while. Whether we fall in love, win the lottery, have a child, or celebrate a victory, the moment of ecstatic transformation that overcomes us provides a glimpse of what we really seek.

But when that moment fades we are left once again focusing on what is missing. Rather, we can learn to identify that feeling of total immersion any time we are willing to give up our judgment of our world and ourselves – when we temporarily move our mental obstacles out of the way of what is an entirely natural feeling that we usually deny ourselves.

As we mature our minds lose the ability to appreciate what we experience and focus instead on what is missing. This is the essential human condition, but what we most want is a feeling. Our ideas about happiness don't create it, but we allow it to ourselves in situations we believe cause it. Nothing and no one can bring happiness to us, not even this book. We return to it only when we decide to bring it to ourselves.

We seek deep feelings to confirm our aliveness. The feeling of happiness doesn't come from circumstances but from moving beyond judging our own reactions.

A simple exercise might help us move in

the right direction. It works much better to do this with a group:

(1) Write down your idea of what you think happiness is. Don't think about this too much. A spontaneous insight is what we are after.

(2) Ask how you can bring that experience into this moment. Again don't think on this for long – allow it to be an intuitive insight if possible rather than a lengthy idea.

(3) Practice doing what you just wrote down at more frequent intervals regardless of the reasons you might be tempted to put in your way.

You will find when you follow the guidelines you created you participate more fully in your activities and interactions. The views and reactions of others may become less significant because you no longer depend on them for feedback, although you may welcome it. You may find that once you are able to allow the experience of happiness to yourself you can bring it into more situations rather than hoping that situations bring it to you.

This is not to say that every moment is an

occasion for happiness. There is sadness in the lives of us all. But more often than not, we bring negativity from other times to our waking moments as a matter of habit rather than of necessity.

When in touch with our happiness we become involved in what we do with our entire being. No one can make us do this or take it away. The goal of our pursuit is not in the future but only can be experienced in this moment.

DEMOCRACY AND AUTOCRACY

Democracy is the political enactment
of a spiritual idea – RAPHAEL WARNOCK

A t the time of the founding of the United States every other country was under autocratic rule. The word "democracy" had not been used for over 2000 years. That term, meaning "rule by the people," came out of ancient Greece, while the Romans later used the word *Libertas*, or freedom, to describe what they considered an essential principle of their republic.

During the US Revolution most people only thought of overthrowing British oppression and had no idea about what would be the best way to govern the new nation. This is typical for revolutions. The US Founders were well-educated and mainly from upper classes. Many were slave holders, yet they considered themselves oppressed by the British

King. They were inspired by such writers as the Englishman John Locke who insisted that people have the right to overthrow oppressive government, and the Frenchman Charles Montesquieu who proposed that a separation of powers of the executive, legislative, and judicial branches of government is needed to keep one branch from becoming too powerful.

At first the US was a loose association of states under the Articles of Confederation. Eleven years later it became clear that a strong central government was required for the nation to succeed and the Constitution was born. Since that time over 100 countries have tried to install democratic governments, many with limited success.

One of the most famous phrases in democracy is from the Declaration of Independence. It states that human beings are entitled to "Life, Liberty and the Pursuit of Happiness." These terms are not well-defined in the fairly short Declaration, but the phrase has inspired people for nearly 250 years to believe that these qualities are their due. We will briefly discuss each in an attempt to clarify what the writers may have had in mind.

We might think the meaning of "Life" to be obvious. But does it simply mean a right to stay alive, or does it refer to a life of quality and recognition for the value of each individual? Most likely everyone who has been inspired by those words would agree it means the latter.

And what is meant by "Liberty?" We can surmise that the term refers to an ability to determine the course of one's own life rather than have major decisions decided by others.

Of these three the phrase that seems to have the least clear meaning is "The Pursuit of Happiness." This was the most fought-over. Did the US Founders intend for denizens of the new country to determine their own paths to the extent possible? Did they assume that the pursuit of happiness was equivalent to freedom?

Most of us probably would agree that democratic governments are more likely than autocracies to afford people an opportunity to pursue happiness. Millions of refugees from autocratic regimes have sought to live in democracies since they came into existence. Those who live under autocracy seek democracy not only for political freedom but because many autocracies lack economic opportunity, and in many the bulk of the population is mired in poverty.

But once we have secured our life and liberty, are we free to pursue happiness? And do those of us fortunate enough to live in democratic countries even agree about what happiness is? Is it the accumulation of goods, involvement in meaningful relationships, or is it freedom to pursue our own path? These are some of the directions that happiness could take. We might also ask if there is an underlying quality that unites our experiences of happiness that lends meaning to the term. And perhaps more importantly, do we have control over our happiness, or are we always at the mercy of the situations of our lives?

Even within what we consider democracies, there are those who would move their countries in the direction of being more autocratic. If we want to preserve democracy it is essential that we identify and combat those elements before they become prevalent.

A group of oligarchs attempted to seize power in ancient Athens, and the Emperor Augustus ended the Roman Republic. In the United States there was an attempt to overthrow the presidential election by an insurrection. Efforts by those of authoritarian minds and their followers always are a threat to "rule by the people." But one person cannot overthrow a government without a large group of followers. So what is it in the human personality that seeks democracy when subject to autocracy, but for many, seeks autocracy when living under democratic rule? Is there a conflict within each person, or just different preferences among different people?

Democracy and autocracy are determined not only by the government in a country or state, but by the nature of its institutions. A truly free country has a free press that explores and exposes shortcomings wherever they find them, including the government. A truly democratic country has a balance between branches of government so that no one person or group can dominate and deprive people of their rights.

A country that intends to maintain democracy has educational institutions that train students in what democracy means. It creates a model for how individual freedom is built by encouraging free and creative expression. Its educational institutions not only train students in the lessons of the past, but encourages them to consider how best to move democracy forward. It exposes them to a variety of views so they can come to their own conclusions about how best to nurture democracy. Clarity about the nature of democracy and how best to preserve it is the greatest lesson our schools can impart.

But above all, democracies that endure have the bulk of their population committed to the idea that "rule by the people" means a government that represents and serves all of the people. Countries where that understanding is not prevalent often have had their democracies overturned.

We who live in democracies see autocrats around us trying to use their influence to permeate the globe. This applies not only to autocratic states, but to countries that pretend to be democratic while moving toward greater oppression. It can be seen in censorship of the press and manipulation of what students are taught.

If we are to preserve our democracies, there must be a clear plan on the part of democratic governments to make a statement that autocratic rule is not permissible. This could include sanctions on leaders put in place on a scale of the degree of freedom a country provides and that hopefully do as little harm as possible to residents. The democratic freedoms of everyone worldwide are connected. If we abandon those who are oppressed anywhere we are opening a gate for the spread of autocracy everywhere.

Going back to the pursuit of happiness, the guarantee of democratic freedoms is an ongoing effort that always will be with us. There is an element in everyone that seeks models for how to act and another element that wants freedom to chart our own course. When we consider those we choose for our leaders it is essential to determine if they are committed to the tenets of democracy, which include recognizing the value of each individual and an appreciation of the potential contribution of everyone. Leaders who denigrate others appeal to the autocratic side of our personality to gain support, and once in power demand allegiance to themselves – even from their followers – rather than to the principle of equal treatment for all.

While we work toward our democratic ideals we can focus on the happiness that democratic government allows us to pursue. If not, the most essential promise of democracy will have been wasted. Understanding what happiness really is and how best to bring it into our lives is not only a worthwhile pursuit but an indispensable element of making democracy work.

FORM
AND ESSENCE

We are stardust, we are golden – JONI MITCHELL

Early in life we seek to identify people and objects in the world around us as we also begin to construct our own identity.

The first form most of us identify is our mother to provide the nourishment we need. We learn to seek her out when we feel hunger or pain. Our groping usually is rewarded and our cries answered, but often it takes insistence to get the attention we want. Children who consistently fail to have their needs met can become discouraged and stop trying.

Later we seek recognition as we continue to learn who we are and whether we are of value to others. Most adults provide nurturant attention to children and validate them with smiles and kind words. But if children do things that adults consider wrong or dangerous they hear the warning in the voices around them which shapes their conduct.

At an early age children enjoy stories of good deeds as they develop ideals about heroic behaviors as models for themselves. They imagine being heroes who rescue those in need and bring good in place of evil. Parents are our early heroes who often seem omnipotent models for how we hope to be someday.

Objects children play with provide forms of expression for their heroic impulses. Creative imagination allows children to practice fantasies about what they might accomplish while imparting the role of guns on sticks and children like themselves on dolls. Very little – or nothing at all – is required to inspire the child's fantasy world.

The essence of our relationships is our need for attachment, but that can take many forms, even that of mistreatment. Children often become attached to their parents regardless of how they are treated. There is a place within that bonds to our early objects of affection that even abused children often maintain. Abusive patterns can substitute for love because it may be all that some children know even though they long for better treatment. They then may continue those patterns in mature relationships because that is the form with which they are most familiar.

Much of the feedback we are given shapes our idea of who we are. If parents or teachers provide assurance that we are capable of accomplishing our goals we are more likely to believe it regardless of any "objective" standards. Of course feedback needs to be given within the realm of where our talents and skills really lie. Negative feedback does not always reflect negatively about what a person is able to accomplish and can be given in a constructive way. I was told to give up my idea of a singing career by my mother, and advised by a science teacher that I do not have the hands of a surgeon; both were right.

As children grow older they begin to take on more worldly heroes and ambitions. Their champions become those who have accomplished much in the areas of sports, acting, music, history or other areas. They begin to model themselves after those who inspire them to excel as they improve their skills.

Although hero worship by children – and many adults – focuses on individuals, it is the essence of what they represent that is attractive. An ability to overcome obstacles, or appeal to members of the opposite sex, or to communicate through music are attractive qualities that represent the fulfilment of fantasies many people hold. We see those who have attained competence, fame or fortune and try to be like them, or relish their accomplishments to enhance our own lives.

Our ultimate aspiration is happiness. Those we admire represent tangible forms of happy and accomplished lives. We live with the myth that people who attain fame and fortune automatically experience fulfillment. But the tragic story of many – often in the entertainment field but in many walks of life – who have destroyed their lives as they discover that reaching the pinnacle of society does not make them happy is common. Many stories of our modern heroes end in self-destructive behaviors or even suicide. So imitating the human forms we worship clearly is not the key to attaining what we most want.

The other types of forms we believe will lead to fulfillment also ultimately fail us. Many who struggle to maintain what society considers successful careers have gaping holes in satisfaction with their lives. Those with considerable wealth we see mentioned in our news media often seem confused, negative or always wanting more. The touted relationships of celebrities we follow so closely often end in blame and recrimination.

So can we separate the forms of happiness we admire from the essence we seek? Can we learn to look past the facades of our heroes and focus on fulfillment rather than forms that often fail to deliver?

Going back to our ideal of a happy childhood may provide some clues, but children often look forward to becoming adults for the fulfillment of their heroic fantasies. So is there an alternative to believing that happiness always is to be found at another time or place, or in the form of another person who does not happen to be us?

Once again, some insight into the way our minds operate may be of value. We are, at least at this period in the history of our planet, a successful species in many ways. But perhaps it is simplistic to measure success simply in terms of survival and domination of the earth.

We not only are a successful species but a compulsive one. For most of our lives we focus on what there is to be done rather than relishing what we have accomplished. And I believe it fair to say that for most of us – including this writer – there is a tendency to look to another time, place or person to find a model for happiness. This has, for the most part, served us well in that we have become the dominant species on earth. Where we often have gone wrong is failing to sublimate our desire to dominate to our ability to appreciate others and the world around us.

For most of us the part that values our lives in the moment and joyfully participates in interaction with others has largely been lost. Perhaps the key to restoring that part of us is to begin being aware of how we defeat ourselves in getting what we truly seek by perpetually focusing on another time and place. Perhaps spending some time away from our habitual quest to focus on the experience of happiness – rather than its pursuit – would allow us to begin restoring the appreciation of life we seek. And perhaps acknowledging the limits of our activities to bring happiness would be a significant step toward its restoration. And perhaps as we become aware of how we habitually pull ourselves out of the moment to focus elsewhere we might find that we land back where we want to be and really always have been but failed to notice.

INSIDE US AND OUT

*It never will be possible by pure reason to arrive
at some absolute truth* – WERNER HEISENBERG

At first we totally engage our surroundings until we begin to think of ourselves as separate beings. Then to function in the world we create an idea of ourselves and try to act within the limits of who we think we are. At times we glimpse a view that reminds us of our connection to what is outside us.

Our concept of separation from others and the world has benefited us from the viewpoint of survival. It allows us to learn at a pace that keeps accelerating. But the size and scope of the universe is so vast that our concepts only are a pale reflection of reality. In science – and our personal lives – concepts based on what we think we know keep changing. Describing the ever-changing reality of nature has been a challenge from the view of science and each of us. Perhaps change is the only word we can use to accurately portray it.

Thus our concepts of the way things are often fail to match reality. We might think we understand how other people act – even those close to us – but still they surprise us. We might believe we know about the world in which we operate every day but often are shocked by how it fails to comply with our preconceptions. The concepts and expectations we have constructed from our experience – and from what we have been told – often fail to accurately predict how our world actually behaves. We are repeatedly reminded that our concepts fall far short of corresponding to reality.

We are taught in school that science has made continual progress in understanding the natural world. But scientific truths have shifted many times and continue to do so with ongoing discoveries. We were taught that if we continue to improve our knowledge we eventually will gain the insights we need to navigate the world and have a successful life. But that understanding never seems to come.

Because of the singular source of all that

exists – called by some the "big bang" and others "creation" – we continue to gaze into the universe to discover more about the origins of our world as well as ourselves. But we cannot absorb what we observe without translating those lessons into concepts. What we learn becomes framed in limited terms that our minds are capable of comprehending. Thus our journey toward knowledge is a venture not only into understanding the universe but into greater awareness of ourselves.

If we accept current scientific theory of the origin of the universe – or the myth of creation in Western religious tradition – we take the view that everything started in one place and continually is expanding. We separate the past in to time periods that correspond to stages in that process. But those are constructs we have created to aid our understanding.

Because of the interactive nature of the universe, in a very real way we are one with all that is around us. We eat and breathe and expel what we don't need as do all plants and animals. Thus we remain part of nature as we take in and let out air and cosmic dust.

We usually see ourselves as outside of nature as we manipulate it to what we think of as our advantage. We have altered the world to benefit ourselves so that we barely notice our connection.

Part of our dilemma is the rigidity of our concepts. We separate the world into convenient divisions to help us understand it. We see a divide between natural and unnatural objects – those created by nature and those engineered by human hands. Among people, we create divisions between those of various backgrounds by color, race, religion, gender, political affiliation and many other categories. Thus we create a separation in our minds between objects and people that are interconnected.

The categories in which we have come to believe do not reflect actuality. Once we have divided the world – and people – into those categories we miss really seeing them. This applies of course to our perceptions of ourselves.

Paying attention to our surroundings and self on an ongoing basis allows us to see more clearly and act less automatically. To do this we must be willing to admit the limits of our current understanding. But that then leads us to a much more accurate understanding.

Because of the limited concepts that are formed in our minds, peering into space is much the same as peering into ourselves. The beauty we see in nature is a reflection of what is inside us. As we become in touch with our inner beauty we then project it onto the universe.

Our judgments of the world and others are based on the expectations we have set. Our disappointment – and even hatred – mainly affect ourselves.

When we are able – at least temporarily – to open our minds to viewing the world beyond our judgments we see that our categories fall short of what really is there. This provides a glimpse of the wisdom we seek. Nothing – and no one – can impart wisdom to us that does not already exist inside.

To speak of justified anger is to say that self-harm is justified. They actually are the same thing. It is only when our anger is expressed that it may or may not affect others.

The experience of happiness reflects a deep acceptance of ourselves which, at the same time, establishes a connection with the world outside of us. Eventually we begin to see that our happiness and unhappiness are not imposed on us but are feelings that are in our realm of control. What holds us back is fear of losing ourselves in an entity that transcends our individuality.

Yet that entity is our true self. As we gain greater comfort in that realization we become more comfortable with all that is within and without.

KNOWLEDGE AND IGNORANCE

Education is not preparation for life;
education is life itself – JOHN DEWEY

At birth we experience a profound connection to all that is around us.

At first we are unable to differentiate between ourselves and what is out there. We watch, grope and grasp until the world comes into focus. We explore what is around us by sound, touch, and taste as concepts of objects and people slowly form in our minds. We soon prioritize our source of nourishment – usually our mothers – as we form our first bond.

We seek knowledge of the world to get what we want. We learn that crying brings the attention we seek. Information comes to us first from our own experience and later from what we are taught.

The way we learn is largely influenced by those around us. Our parents can encourage us to explore and come to our own conclusions to the extent possible, or impose their ideas of what is true – including who and what is good and bad – on our forming minds. They need to protect us from danger in our exploratory years until we incorporate those lessons into our own views. We hear the emotional content of their alarm as they tell us "the stove is hot" and that lesson becomes part of our model of the world.

As we approach maturity we gain a clearer image of reality. We imitate not only the words, but the attitudes that parents, teachers and others impart to us. If we are taught to keep an open mind we will become more confident in forming our own conclusions about others and the world. If we are taught that some people or groups are superior or inferior, we will maintain that lesson in our minds and it will govern our actions.

By adolescence we may think we have an accurate picture of reality, but soon become disillusioned as we discover the limits of our understanding. We begin to see that everything we were told may not be true. We decide whether to stick with the ideas we have been taught in order to keep our world simple, or open ourselves to a search for greater understanding.

We continue to rely on others to provide guidance about what is true and how to act. But those ideas are based on their limited perspectives. We are subjected to conflicting views which often leads to confusion, but we adopt a self-image to allow us to function in the world. Our doubts often bring discomfort and uncertainty, so we would rather embrace simple views than deal with our confusion.

Some of those we know exhibit an uncanny confidence in their views and actions. They provide what seems like islands of stability in an unstable world. When unsure of ourselves we follow them, often to unforeseen places.

But if we are paying attention we begin to see that very few of our ideas and actions actually lead to fulfillment. What we are told will bring satisfaction – financial gain, relationships, leisure activities – fail to work beyond the short term. If we are honest with ourselves we admit to uncertainty about whether there is anything we can do to bring ourselves the happiness or sense of inner peace we seek.

Sometimes we want to give up in our hope that we will attain the wisdom and understanding we once assumed would allow us to successfully navigate the world. We may enter into despair about whether anything can work to end our dilemma – other than denial that it exists – so we can carry on the daily routines of our lives. But somehow there remains a gnawing underlying lack of fulfillment.

At times we glimpse something larger. We feel connected to others and the world when we experience success in career or competition, or just enjoy the company of people. But often we feel isolated and disconnected. Our connections become limited to who and what we consider worthy of our time and efforts. We settle into a pattern of certainty about the limited world we have created for ourselves and do our best to ignore the uncertainty inside.

But our certainty has a cost.

Our lives become a pale reflection of the life we hoped to live. The enthusiasm that once energized us becomes sublimated to just getting by. The spark that motivated us no longer seems ignited. We engage others and the world with a facade of having figured it all out but often find ourselves disengaged in any meaningful way.

We seek understanding via media or reading but they only grant temporary insight. Music and other arts sometimes provide a sense of fulfillment greater than words.

Most of us believe there is no other approach than the pattern into which we have settled. We have forgotten the joy and engagement with which we once greeted others and the world.

Our knowledge may lead to better health and an expanded life span but it never leads to happiness because it falls short of understanding how to bring it about. This provides us a choice about continuing to pretend that our lives are satisfying or admitting that they fall short.

One possible route is acknowledging our ignorance, to ourselves if not to others. When willing to concede how little we know about what brings meaning to life, we land at the same level as everyone else. We then are forced to interact with the world in a spirit of humility. But as we do this we begin to see more clearly than we can by the filters of our concepts. We experience a more complete connection with a world of which we now begin to realize we are not above or below but just a part.

In each age of the history of humanity we have thought our knowledge and insights to be superior to any preceding period. We think we know much now, but that always has been the case. When we look back 50 or 100 years we can see how little people knew then. 50 and 100 years from now people will look back at our ignorance and how we live in innocent times.

As our civilizations become more advanced we remain in a medieval mindset. We are beset by preconceptions and prejudices that keep us – at least as individuals – from seeing others and our world with much clarity. We categorize people in ways that fail to allow us the genuine interactions we seek.

No matter how long we stay in school, or how hard we study the world around us, or how much we think we know, reality is infinitely larger than any level of understanding we can attain. As our concepts continue to fall short, all we can be confident of is that we really know nothing.

That leaves us at the same level of everyone else, except that admitting our ignorance gives us a clearer view than we had when our minds were full of knowledge. But it is that clearer view we have been seeking all along.

LIFE AND DEATH

*The Self, which dwells in the body of everyone, is
eternal and never can be slain* – BHAGAVAD GITA

At a very early age we learn to divide the
world into what is alive and what is not.
But science – and our own observations – tell
us it is not that simple.

We can see that plants and animals come
from the earth and return to it. But many of
us hope or believe that for people there is a
consciousness that continues after death.

A question we might consider is whether
the real self is the body or that part of us
that observes what happens to us and the
world. Are we a physical entity that intercon-
nects with what is around us like plants and
other creatures, or are we the consciousness
that reads these words and contemplates our
nature?

In our daily functioning we think of ourselves as separate entities. Although aware
that our body ultimately will die, our main

focus is that we need to be fed, make a living, hopefully experience love, and perhaps propagate ourselves.

Most of us rarely think about our relationship to that which sustains us unless it becomes threatened. We don't regularly concern ourselves with whether the food and drink we consume and the air we breathe will no longer be there. Instead we focus on the daily activities of our lives.

But many ancient tribes – and some remote ones in our day – considered the entire world around them as sacred, imbued with spirits and very much alive. In many religions gratefulness to the power that sustains us is part of everyday living. In some traditions, such as that expressed by the Bhagavad Gita, an essential Hindu text, the entire universe, including what we usually consider the separate self, is subsumed in a larger Self of which we all are part.

So in different cultures the idea of life and death varies from our own. Some consider people to be entities interconnected with the world and others consider them separate. The

words we use, which refer primarily to individual people and objects, tend to enforce the
second view. But by observation, and some
consideration of what we have observed, a
different view might emerge that sheds some
light on our search for fulfillment.

Consider the potato. Those of us who have
them in our kitchen – perhaps all of us – find
that they begin changing form if not used in
a fairly short period of time. The origin of
the potato is dirt – as is the case for all living things – and we easily can accept that it
begins in dirt and returns to it. In our minds
– and this is fortunate – we have an idealized
form of the potato: round and usually brown,
red or white. When it approaches this form
we consider it fit to eat. In its stages before
and after we might think of it as a tuber. The
reality is that there is a continually changing
entity that passes into and out of the form we
call potato. We don't have an adequate way
to describe its changing form but continual
change is closer to reality than any one phase
we can easily consider. There are no words in
our vocabulary to describe the forms the poor

potato goes through perhaps except by using the word "change" itself.

It's not only the potato that is continually in flux, but so is every living being, including ourselves. Considering what geologists have discovered and tell us, that also is true of our world and the universe that surrounds us. Thus our words and ideas of who we are fall short of describing what really happens; reality is that flux that our words only approach and never adequately describe.

Going back to the origins of the universe, science now tells us that what surrounds us began with a sudden act that some call a "bang" and some refer to as creation. Since that time – and perhaps in the period leading up to it – there has been continual change and evolution for everything in our universe. It may not be accurate to describe that ongoing activity as resulting in "people" and "things" because all continually is in the process of change. But for us to survive and function, thinking of objects and ourselves as separate entities has served us well. If our functional understanding is based on a fiction, it is that fiction that has allowed us to thrive.

As individuals we hope to survive, but mere survival never is enough for us to experience happiness. We want stability in our lives so that we don't need to continually struggle to get our needs met. But in our minds that stability rarely occurs – it usually is projected to be in some other time or place.

We hold on to standards for our lives and world to meet before we allow ourselves happiness. Our work needs to be more than just a job, we want it to be a satisfying occupation. Our relationships must be more than just functional, they must bring us a sense of recognition. Our recreational activities must bring us enjoyment. We thus remain dependent on others and the world for happiness and rarely take responsibility for bringing it to ourselves.

But if we shift our view to take into account the true nature of our physical being there only is change and no real death. This view, of course, will not work well for survival. We still need to engage in our activities as individuals to survive and hopefully thrive.

But from the viewpoint of who we really are – nature and the universe itself – change is our most basic self and always will be. We can carry this consciousness with us regardless of the everyday struggles in which we engage as individuals.

From the viewpoint of our consciousness – the part that observes and describes our nature – there only is ongoing change. It is a continuing witness to the flux around us, and that is beyond the words by which we describe our world.

So from the viewpoint of reality – which is the change that began at the inception of the universe and continues through and beyond this moment – it makes no sense to hold on to our ideal of how we want the world to be before we allow ourselves happiness. As we begin to see this we can let go of our continual need for the circumstances of our lives to be different than they are, which is a never-ending thought process that keeps us from an experience of contentment.

We might think it impossible to hold both perspectives in our minds. But the viewpoint of the connectedness of all things – which is the best way we can describe what really exists – is that with which we started. We long to return to that view but in fact it never left us. We can keep it in mind as we go about our daily activities, knowing that they cannot lead to the happiness that already is our ongoing condition.

PAST, PRESENT AND FUTURE

The future belongs to those who believe in the beauty of their dreams – ELEANOR ROOSEVELT

The past and future merge in the present, which is the only time in which we can do anything.

Time is a continuum, but we divide the past into incidents that allow us to better understand it. Our descriptions of events represent memories of an ongoing reality that proceeds right up to the present and beyond. We have a preference for how the past should have been – people should have treated us better or we should have acted better or the circumstances of our lives should have been better. We cling to our resentment and regret.

Our science, history and memories tell us that the past exists. We see traces of it everywhere. But our idea of the past also is based on selective memory. We determine which incidents are meaningful to us in our own time, such as the pathos of past wars and how we should never repeat them, yet we repeat them. Other memories invoke nostalgia for what we think of as better times. But in no period have we ever exclaimed: "These are the best of times," because we always think of the best times as being in the past or future.

There is a tyranny of the past over our current lives and times. We believe that past incidents determine the quality of our lives as we relive them in our minds. But our focus on the past, rather than on our vision for the future, is what keeps us stuck there in the present.

We hold ideals in our minds in which we compare past actions by ourselves or others with what we think should have been done. We regret having acted in a way that caused someone harm or we dwell on anger in a belief that others harmed us.

Alternately we have memories of good times that meet our ideals and evoke a sense of happiness in the present. But much of our idea of the past is based on nostalgia for an idealized time that never existed, just as we idealize a future utopian time when we will have stopped reliving the past.

Our ideas about the past also shape our intent for the future, including how we educate our children. If we want to shape a future generation of children who treat each other fairly, we teach them to acknowledge each other and respect their individuality. Then we model that type of behavior. If we prefer a future generation that ignores injustice, we avoid teaching them about inequities of the past.

We want to move beyond our self-destructive habits of the past, whether overindulgence or overreaction. We believe we never will be happy until we release ourselves from our actions that harm ourselves and others. Yet habits by which we harm others and ourselves continue.

We are convinced that a behavior begets similar behavior; that our past determines who we are and how we act. But there is no such law. We can move beyond the view that our fate is determined by factors beyond our control.

Many studies show that animals and children that are mistreated exhibit signs of trauma throughout their lives. But other studies show that children who are mistreated can recover. These are testaments to human resilience.

In the best of circumstances – even when people are treated well – they still can choose to dwell on what they consider negative influences from their past. Similarly, when treated poorly, we can slowly learn to bring to ourselves the nurturance we believe missing from our lives.

In moments when we treat others well we experience being treated well. When we were young there was no substitute for the healing care of our mothers. But now we can bring empathy to ourselves for the mental wounds that dwell within.

Doing this takes practice over time. When we notice that we are dwelling on our pain we can begin to bring ourselves the empathy we seek. We can allow our feeling to be there and the more we are able to do that the more likely it will eventually leave us. Feelings that are fully felt tend to move on by themselves.

Happiness is not about always being in a "happy" place. It also is about allowing ourselves to be in whatever place we are – about not continually trying to get out of our feelings. It is not so much about smiling as having someone smile upon us. And sometimes the only person willing to smile upon us is ourselves. As we do this we find ourselves more fully in the present moment where we most long to be.

US AND THEM

He who fears he will suffer already suffers
what he fears – MICHEL DE MONTAIGNE

As we mature we divide the world into what is inside of us and what is outside in our minds. We begin to believe that who and what is around us affects our happiness and unhappiness.

As we engage with others – parents, siblings, teachers, friends – we learn behaviors we hope will get our physical and psychological needs met. We receive continual input about what works and what does not; what we can do and what we cannot. We learn who is part of our family and tribe and who is not, and often come to believe that those outside our group are not quite as "human" as those who are part of it.

There are two types of interactions. One is when we interact to gain advantage over others; the second is when we interact to benefit ourselves and others at the same time. In times of genuine happiness we feel ourselves in harmony with others; we experience satisfaction in treating them well. But when we interact with those we have labeled as the "other" – out loud or in our minds – we bring upon ourselves a feeling of distrust and discomfort although we may be unaware we have done this.

We have a model in our minds for how we should be treated and hold a high standard for the consideration we expect and think we deserve. We often are beset by anger at the way others treat us. Our daily interactions are filled with what we think of as rudeness by those we encounter. Yet others may have no idea we are harboring resentment, thus the discontent we hold in our minds hurts mainly ourselves.

Our dilemma is how to get others and the world to meet our expectations so we can experience the happiness we seek.

We long to return to the interactions we believe we had when very young. But this became more difficult as we began considering ourselves separate beings with clear ideas of the limits between us and others.

Experiences of both nurturance and disappointment are stored in our minds and affect our subsequent interactions. When others extend support to us we may or may not notice due to our resentment from having been treated poorly in the past. But when we extend kindness and consideration to others – regardless of their awareness or acceptance of our gesture – we experience kindness for ourselves.

We may not know what is going on in the minds of others. People often don't discuss their moods but instead act them out. We might believe we know what they are thinking but what seems like inconsideration may or may not be intentional. All we know of others is the image of them we hold in our minds and our response to that image. When we treat others kindly we experience kindness; when we treat others disrespectfully we experience disrespect. As we treat others as less than human, we also experience being less than human due to the disconnection we create between us.

When we really pay attention we can become more aware of the feelings we create for ourselves. We begin to see how we manufacture our experience of happiness or unhappiness and then bring that into our interactions. We can allow incidents of distress and anger to move through us rather than hanging on to them. That way of interacting is most natural to us. As we do this we begin to see that our real self is the part of us who observes what happens rather than the person who is buffeted by the circumstances of our lives. This is when peace of mind comes upon us.

Our tribalism affects all areas of our lives – both the personal and political. Our rivalries build in our minds to divide our regions, countries and world into those we believe are on our side and those who are against us. This is the origin of the wars that have plagued humanity for all time.

Going back into prehistory there is much evidence of war and rivalry between groups. The central myth of the Ancient Greeks was the Trojan War that was reflected in the plays that have come down to us. Native Americans slaughtered and enslaved their enemies. Our unwillingness to consider the "other" as human has guided our political interactions as long as history has been written.

But rivalries also have been overcome to create cooperation. North American Indians created a Council of Peace in the 1700s. The League of Nations and United Nations were formed to forge international cooperation. Europeans designed the European Union which has brought them greater prosperity.

Ultimately we forge connections that are positive or negative. As we interact we assume the worst or best of others. It is not unusual to change our view of the same individual over the course of a relationship.

If we rely on others to determine the positive or negative nature of our relationships we are dependent on them for our state of mind. But if we bring a recognition for the essence of the other into our interactions we experience the acknowledgment we seek.

So in a very real way there is no "us" and "them." There only is the decision on the part of each of us to recognize the essential core of who we are and bring that into our interactions, or choose not to do this. As we do we bring ourselves the recognition we seek.

If you think that is not the way most people function you would be right. But the democratic ideal of the recognition of the value of every human being also was a bold step forward. It is up to each of us – as individuals – to bring this empathetic way of being into our everyday interactions if only for the selfish reason that it allows us the lives we want and also moves us toward creating the world we want.

We will fail at this effort often and often succeed. But we must keep on trying. The alternative is to give up altogether which we know at the core of our being we never can do.

Ours is an age of shifting values when many feel adrift in a changing world. Because of the difficulty of young people in becoming secure in finding their essential self it is especially crucial to acknowledge the value of youths we encounter. Assuring them of their validity can provide an anchor as they continue to engage in a search for their values and beliefs. It also is important to remember that as we extend compassion to others we experience compassion for ourselves.

Above all, we each are human. We want to be recognized for our humanity as well as our individuality. As we acknowledge the validity of others – regardless of their backgrounds or beliefs – we bring it to ourselves.

WHAT EVERYBODY WANTS

Whoever is happy will make others happy too
– ANNE FRANK

The feeling we had when born was one of immersion in all that is around us.

But in that immersion we had no idea of the separateness that our words would eventually force us to accept. It only was later when we emerged from that way of being that we felt something missing in our lives.

The love and acceptance that everyone wants – first represented by our mothers and later by others – is a wish to return to that connected self. But seeking that state only perpetuates the myth in our minds that we are not already connected.

All that is left is for us to move past the words we use every day – and even past the words you read here – to allow ourselves to suspend our myth of separateness and acknowledge that the connection we seek already is reality. That only becomes meaningful when it is experienced as felt and not just as a concept.

True happiness is simply the unconditional acknowledgment of the beauty and infiniteness of who we are. We wait all our lives for permission to feel this – from financial gain, from relationships, from a sunset, from us or our team or country winning – but ultimately it only happens when we are willing to grant it to ourselves.

In this moment – and every moment – only you can provide what you most want. The moment you begin seeking it you are denying it to yourself.

If you are fortunate enough to live in a country that allows the "pursuit of happiness" your ability to acknowledge your real condition will be enhanced by sharing these ideas with others. But discussing our real nature is difficult in the best of circumstances because of the structure of the language we have created that otherwise has served us well.

That language divides our view of our

world and selves into separate units that don't exist objectively. Science and religion tell us we are composed of the elements of the universe that continually pass into us and out. Thus our unity with all that exists already is established.

Nevertheless we play the "game of existence." This is how we have evolved as individuals and our civilizations have advanced. But knowing who we really are as we play makes the game much more enjoyable and takes the seeking out of our everyday tasks. As we dwell in that space life becomes much more of a joy than a struggle. But then we forget and think that the struggle is real.

Denying our true nature of connectedness leads to competition where cooperation would work much better to meet our needs. It also has led to endless disputes between individuals and war between nations. Perhaps a worthy guideline for how to act in times of strife might be to remember that what we do to others we do to ourselves in the moment we act.

So all we can do is read books like this and have discussions with those who are willing to acknowledge the reality in which we all dwell. That reality also is from where we have come and to where we shall return. We have dwelled in it as long as time has existed and will continue to dwell there for all time to come.

ABOUT THE AUTHOR

Steve Zolno graduated from Shimer College with a bachelor's degree in Social Sciences and holds a master's in Educational Psychology from Sonoma State University. Steve has founded and directed private schools and a health care agency in the San Francisco Bay Area. He is the author of five previous books.